# Cookii
## Chr

CW00530152

To Simon and me, Christ the exchange of pretty, ............ packages beside a decorated tree, and food to be enjoyed with friends and family. Most of us remember fondly, the traditional foods which our mothers, aunts and grandmothers produced each year.

If you go shopping in December, you are sure to find a wide variety of "Christmassy" foods, attractively wrapped. When you look at the price tags on these packages, however, you will probably be shocked.

We have found that we can make and package attractively, for a much more reasonable price, gifts which our friends and relations will really enjoy.

We hope that the recipes in this book will inspire you! Many of the foods may be made some time before Christmas.

A few of the recipes may require special skills, but many are suitable for children to make, with a little help from you to start with. We hope that you will encourage children to make such things.

For really attractive gifts, consider your containers, wrapping and presentation. Consider re-useable containers such as glasses, decorative jars, baskets and boxes. If your containers do not have lids, cover them with cling wrap etc.

Make good use of ribbons etc., and try to make some really attractive bows. If you don't know how to curl the ends of long ribbons to form "corkscrews," ask a friend who knows how, to show you.

We hope that you enjoy making a number of the recipes from this book, giving them to friends, and enjoying them with your families.

Happy Cooking

**Simon & Alison Holst**

# Lemon Herb Roasted Chicken

Turkey may be traditional, but a big roast chicken (or two) is just as delicious – and far more economical! Surrounded with stuffing balls and the usual trimmings it really looks the part too.

## For 6–8 servings:

1 size 20–24 chicken (thawed)

2 Tbsp olive oil

4 cloves garlic, peeled

1–2 Tbsp chopped basil

1 Tbsp chopped rosemary

finely grated zest 1 lemon

1 lemon

2 cloves garlic, crushed

1 cup couscous

1 cup boiling water

1 tsp chicken stock

1 Tbsp oil

1 medium onion, diced

¼ cup pinenuts

¼ cup each chopped dried apricots and cranberries

¼ cup chopped herbs

1 large egg

**1** Preheat the oven to 180°C.

**2** Blend the oil, two cloves of the garlic, herbs and lemon zest together. Wash and pat dry the chicken. Rub about 2 tsp of the herb puree into the cavity, cut several slashes in the zested lemon then crush the remaining garlic and stuff these into the cavity. Place the chicken in a baking paper-lined roasting pan, then rub the skin with the remaining herb mixture.

**3** Place the roasting pan in the middle of the preheated oven and roast for about 2 hours or until the juices run clear when the thigh is pierced at the thickest part. Remove from the oven and rest for 5–10 minutes before carving.

## Stuffing Balls

**1** Place the couscous in a large bowl. Add the boiling water and instant stock, stir, then cover and leave to stand for about 5–10 minutes. Meanwhile heat the oil in a medium-sized frypan and sauté the onion until soft, then stir in the pinenuts and cook, stirring frequently until the nuts are lightly coloured.

**2** Add the onion mixture and remaining ingredients to the soaked couscous and stir to combine. Shape the mixture into eight balls, then arrange these around the chicken for the last hour of cooking.

# Baked Glazed Ham

**Many New Zealand families buy a ham to eat over the holiday period. Of course a ham is just fine served 'as is' but if you want it to look really special, why not try glazing it?**

1 medium-large ham

about 20g whole cloves

**Glaze**

½ cup brown sugar

½ cup orange or pineapple juice

1–2 Tbsp wholegrain mustard

½–1 tsp ground cloves

**❶** Heat the oven to 150°C. Measure the glaze ingredients into a frypan or pot. Heat to boiling then simmer, stirring frequently, until the mixture has thickened a little, then remove from the heat.

**❷** Place the ham on a clean board. Starting at the cut end, slide your fingers just under the skin, loosening it from the flesh and fat until you can remove it from most of the surface (leave a little at the shank end if desired).

**❸** Score the surface of the ham diagonally (cutting just through the fat) in two directions to create a diamond pattern. Press a clove into the centre of each diamond.

**❹** Place the ham in a large, foil and/or baking paper lined roasting pan. Brush the surface generously with the glaze. Put the roasting pan in the oven (so the top of the ham is as close to the middle of the oven as size will allow). Bake for 1½–2 hours, brushing the surface of the ham with remaining glaze and/or pan drippings every 20–30 minutes. (It may also pay to rotate the pan once or twice for even browning too.) If the surface appears to be browning too fast, reduce the heat to 125°C.

**❺** Place hot or warm ham on a serving platter and serve. Once cooled, refrigerate and store the leftovers as you would an unglazed ham.

# Peter's Special Cake

This is a lovely, dark, moist, fruity cake. It contains no essences. We like to add a mixture of spices, but we don't use very much of any of these. You can leave out those you do not have.

**For one 23cm square or round cake:**

500g sultanas

500g raisins

500g currants

½ cup sherry

rind of 1 lemon

rind of 1 orange

1½ cups brown sugar

250g butter, softened

1 Tbsp treacle

5 eggs

2 cups flour

½ tsp each ground allspice, cardamom, cinnamon, cloves, coriander and nutmeg

1. One to two days before the cake is made, put the dried fruits into a plastic bag with the sherry. Turn the bag every now and then. Leave the bag in a warm place until all the sherry has been absorbed by the fruit.

2. Remove the coloured rind of the lemon and orange with a potato peeler. Process with the sugar until very finely chopped. Add butter, process until soft and fluffy then add the treacle and mix again. Add eggs, one at a time, with a tablespoon of the measured flour between each. Mix the rest of the flour and the spices with the fruit in a very large bowl.

3. Tip the creamed mixture into the floured fruit, and mix until soft enough to drop from your hand. If the mixture is too dry, add up to ¼ cup of extra sherry or spirits.

4. Put the mixture into a 23cm round or square tin lined with greaseproof paper. Decorate top with almonds or cherries if you like.

5. Bake at 150°C for one hour, then at 140°C for about 3 hours, until a skewer in the centre comes out clean.

6. If you like, dribble ¼ cup rum or brandy over it while it is very hot.

7. Leave an hour before removing from the tin.

# Pineapple Christmas Cake

For many years Alison's rich pineapple cake has been made to celebrate Christmas, by families all around the country. It is the most used of all her rich cake recipes.

**For one 23cm cake, two 18cm cakes or 12 (mini) 10cm cakes:**

1.5kg mixed fruit*

450g can crushed pineapple

3 cups flour

1 tsp each cinnamon and mixed spice

½ tsp ground cloves

225g butter

1 cup sugar

½ tsp each vanilla, almond and lemon essences

6 large eggs

up to 1 extra cup of flour

about 50g glacé cherries and 50g blanched almonds for decoration

* Choose only very good quality mixed fruit. If this is not available, replace with 700g sultanas, 500g raisins, 250g currants and 50g mixed peel.

**1** Two or three days before mixing the cake, put the mixed fruit in a large (unperforated) oven bag or plastic bag with the undrained pineapple. Leave in a warm place, turning the bag occasionally, until all the juice is absorbed.
**Note:** To make cake immediately, discard liquid from pineapple. Wash, then dry the fruit the same day that you mix the cake. You are unlikely to need the extra flour.

**2** Mix the spices with 3 cups flour and put aside. Cream the butter, sugar and essences until light and smooth. Beat in eggs, one at a time, adding about 2 tablespoons of the spiced flour with each egg. Toss together the prepared fruit and the remaining spiced flour in a large bowl or a roasting pan. Stir in the creamed mixture using a wooden spoon or your hand.

**3** The mixture should be just soft enough to drop from your hand. If it seems too soft, add more flour. Press mixture into paper-lined tin(s), levelling the top(s).

**4** Decorate with blanched almonds and cherries if you do not plan to ice the cake.

**5** Bake 23cm cake at 150°C for 1½ hours, then at 130°C for about 2 hours longer. Bake 18cm cakes at 140°C for 1 hour, then at 130°C for about an hour longer. Bake mini cakes (225-250g each) at 130°C for about 1½ hours. (Use paper-lined, well cleaned fish cans.)

**6** Cakes are cooked when a skewer pushed to base of middle of the cake comes out clean. Sprinkle cake(s) with ¼ cup brandy or sherry, if you like. Remove cake(s) from tin(s) when cold.

# Golden Christmas Cake

**This interesting Christmas cake has rapidly become one of Alison's most requested recipes! It is lighter in colour than most traditional Christmas cakes, and very pretty.**

### For a 23cm round or square (2.25kg) cake:

about 1 cup each cubed crystallised mango, papaya, pineapple and melon

1 cup sultanas

1 cup dried cranberries or extra sultanas

1 cup white wine

½–1 cup glacé cherries, optional

250g butter

1 cup sugar

5 large eggs

1 cup ground almonds

1 tsp vanilla essence

½ tsp almond essence

grated rind of 1 orange and lemon

1½ cups high grade flour

1½ tsp baking powder

❶ Buy a total of about 1kg of 3 or 4 of the crystallised fruits. Cut these into 5mm cubes with scissors or a sharp knife. Add the sultanas and cranberries to the crystallised fruit. Simmer the fruit and wine in a covered frypan for five minutes or until nearly all liquid is absorbed, then leave to stand in the covered pan overnight or for 8 hours to soak up remaining liquid. (Fruit will have a beautiful jewel-like appearance!) Stir in the quartered cherries, if using.

❷ Heat oven to 150°C (140°C fanbake), with the rack just below the middle. Prepare a 23cm round or square pan, lining sides and base with baking paper or a Teflon liner.

❸ In a food processor or large bowl, beat the soft (but not melted) butter and sugar until creamy. Beat in one egg at a time, adding a spoonful of the ground almonds after each one. Beat in the essences, remaining ground almonds and the finely grated citrus rinds, then sift in the flour and baking powder. Combine the cake mixture and the cold, prepared fruit using your hand and spread mixture evenly in the prepared pan.

❹ Bake at 150°C (140°C fanbake) for 45 minutes then at 130°C (120°C fanbake) for 1½–2 hours. The cake is cooked when a skewer pushed deeply in the centre comes out clean.

❺ When cooled, wrap loosely with baking paper, then refrigerate. For best flavour, leave a week before eating. Serve as is, or ice with almond Icing and Royal or Plastic Icing.

# Easy-mix Fruit and Rum Cake

Here is a cake of modest size, which is very little trouble to put together. Its wonderful flavour comes from the dark raisins and the rum used in it — it contains no essences or spices at all.

**For one 20cm square or round cake:**

1kg small dark (Californian) raisins

½ cup liquid (see right)

200g butter

2 cups flour

1 cup sugar

1 tsp baking soda

½ tsp salt

¼ cup golden syrup

½ cup milk

2 large eggs

**1** Put the raisins in an unpunctured plastic bag with ½ cup of rum or a mixture of sherry and rum and leave the fruit to stand in it for 24–48 hours, until the fruit has soaked up all the liquid.

**2** Cut or rub the cold butter into the flour, sugar, baking soda and salt, using a food processor, a pastry blender, or your fingers.

**3** Measure the syrup in a measure preheated with very hot water, warm the syrup and milk just enough to combine them, beat in the eggs, then mix this liquid, the prepared fruit and the dry mixture together.

**4** If you do not intend to ice your cake, decorate the top with a pattern of blanched almonds, cherries etc.

**5** Bake in a lined 20cm square tin at 150°C for 2¼–2½ hours, until a skewer inserted in the centre, pushed down to the bottom comes out clean.

**6** If you have decorated the top of the cake with nuts, "polish" them by rubbing a little oil on the palm of your hand, and rubbing your hand over the surface of the cake until the nuts shine.

# Home-made Almond Icing

Almond icing is easy to make. This is enough for a medium sized cake. Double the quantity if you want enough for a very thick layer, for icing down the sides, or for marzipan fruit.

100g ground almonds

1 cup icing sugar

½ cup caster sugar

1 egg yolk

2 Tbsp lemon juice, strained

¼ tsp almond essence, optional

**1** Combine the ground almonds and sugars in a food processor or mixing bowl. Mix the egg yolk with half of the lemon juice and add to the almond mixture with a little almond essence if desired.

**2** Add remaining lemon juice, a little at a time, until you make a paste that is easy to roll out.

**3** Warm a little apricot jam, sieve, and brush over the cake, then roll out the almond paste on a dry board sprinkled with icing sugar. Place over the cake smoothly, using a rolling pin.

# Royal Icing

The top coat of icing on a fruit cake is sometimes made of Royal icing, rather than plastic icing. Royal icing is very white, sets hard and is easy to pipe into rosettes, lines, dots, etc.

1 egg white

1 tsp lemon juice, strained

½ tsp glycerine, optional

2 cups sifted icing sugar

**1** In a food processor or bowl, mix the egg white and lemon juice only until frothy. Add the icing sugar a few tablespoons at a time, mixing well between additions. Stop when the icing is the consistency you want. Mix in glycerine.

**2** Use the icing immediately, or store it in an airtight bag for up to two or three days. For piping, thin down with a little water if necessary.

**Notes:** If you want to pipe royal icing into elaborate shapes such as leaves and roses, buy icing sugar that does not contain cornflour. Glycerine is supposed to keep royal icing softer than it would be otherwise, but it is not essential.

# Kirsten's Christmas Biscotti

This loaf looks festive, is relatively quick to make, and the recipe produces a large number of pieces. A few slices in a small cellophane bag, tied with pretty curling ribbon, make a good small gift.

**For a loaf 9 x 23cm:**

3 eggs

½ tsp salt

½ cup sugar

¼ tsp almond essence

½ tsp vanilla essence

finely grated rind of 1 orange

1 cup flour

1½ cups raw almonds or 1 cup raw almonds plus ½ cup pistachio nuts

1½ cups red glacé cherries

**1** Beat the eggs, salt, sugar and essences until light and fluffy, then add the finely grated orange rind.

**2** Mix the flour, almonds and cherries together, then fold them into the egg mixture.

**3** Turn mixture into a loaf tin about 9x23x8 cm, lined with a Teflon liner or buttered baking paper, making sure that the top is evenly flattened. Bake at 180°C for 45–50 minutes, or until loaf is lightly browned and the centre springs back when pressed.

**4** When cool, remove from tin, wrap and refrigerate for at least 24 hours, then cut into about 40 thin slices with a sharp, serrated knife.

**5** Bake slices on a lined oven tray at 125°–150°C for about 30 minutes, until the slices colour slightly. Cool on racks then store in airtight containers until required.
**Note:** If you want a multi-coloured loaf, use cherries of mixed colours, some red and some green.

**6** If you use unblanched almonds, they will be more noticeable in the loaf.

# Panforte

This chewy, very firm, dark and compact festive cake is of Italian origin. It contains no baking powder or eggs. Wedges or rectangular pieces, attractively gift-wrapped, make a special gift.

**For about 12–15 servings:**

1 cup blanched almonds

1 cup hazelnuts

1 cup pecans

¼ cup caster sugar

½ cup honey

1 cup mixed fruit

½ cup crystallised ginger

½ cup standard (plain) flour

¼ cup cocoa

2 tsp cinnamon

75g butter

½ cup chocolate chips

**1** Heat the oven to 150°C, with the rack just below the middle. Line a 24cm round or a 23cm square pan with baking paper.

**2** Lightly roast all the nuts together in a large shallow baking dish in the oven as it heats, checking every few minutes.

**3** Put the sugar and honey in a frypan ready to heat later. Roughly chop the ginger and stir it through the mixed fruit. Sift the flour, cocoa and cinnamon together and set aside.

**4** Melt the butter and chocolate chips together in a large bowl in the microwave oven at 50% power for about 2 minutes, or over a pot of hot water. When the almonds are a light beige colour and when the other nuts are ready stir them into the melted chocolate mixture.

**5** Warm the sugar and honey together over low to moderate heat, stirring until the sugar dissolves. When the mixture bubbles all over the surface, pour it into the chocolate and nut mixture. Add the sifted flour mixture and the mixed fruit and stir until everything is evenly blended.

**6** Pour the warm mixture into the prepared pan then pat out evenly.

**7** Bake for 30–45 minutes or until the centre is as cooked as the outer edges. The hot cake becomes much firmer on cooling. Leave it in a cool place for at least 24 hours before cutting in wedges or rectangles with a sharp knife. Store in an airtight jar.

# Traditional Christmas Mincemeat

Alison has never yet tasted bought Christmas mincemeat which could hold a candle to the mixture she makes herself. She has made this easy recipe ever since she bought her first food processor. It is a modification of her mother's recipe, but contains no suet, so it can be eaten raw as well as cooked.

rind of 1 lemon

rind of 1 orange

1 cup brown sugar

3 small Braeburn apples

juice of 1 lemon

2 cups sultanas

2 cups mixed fruit

1 tsp cinnamon

1 tsp mixed spice

1 tsp grated nutmeg

1 tsp salt

½ tsp ground cloves

¼ cup brandy, whisky or rum

**1** Remove all the coloured rind from the lemon and orange with a potato peeler, then chop with the sugar in the food processor until very fine.

**2** Add the chunks of unpeeled apple, lemon juice, half the sultanas and half the mixed fruit. Process until apple is finely chopped.

**3** Add remaining fruit and flavourings, and process again, briefly without mushing.

**4** Spoon into jars which have been boiled for 3–4 minutes, and top with a little more spirits. Top with boiled screw tops, and refrigerate up to a year, adding more spirits if the mixture becomes dry.

# Christmas Mincemeat Pies

If you have time, turn some of your Christmas mincemeat into mince pies before you get too busy with other festive tasks, and hide them in the freezer. When time is short, make filo triangles instead. This mixture is easy to work with, although it takes some time to shape. It makes pies that freeze and reheat well.

**Pastry**

100g butter

½ cup sugar

1 egg

1 cup flour

1 cup self-raising flour

**1** Soften but do not melt butter. Beat in sugar and egg until well combined. Stir in unsifted flours and mix well to form a dough. If too dry, add a little milk. If too soft to work with, refrigerate rather than adding more flour.

**2** Lightly flour a board to prevent sticking and roll out the pastry.

**3** Using a glass, round lid or fluted cutter, cut out the circles for the bottom of the pies (size will depend on the muffin pans in which the pies will be baked). The circles for the tops are cut with a smaller cutter or, if available, small biscuit cutters which form hearts, stars, diamonds, etc.

**4** Ease the dough into medium or mini muffin pans, then spoon in the mincemeat mixture and top with the smaller shapes or circles of pastry, pressing the edges lightly.

**5** Bake at 170°–180°C for 10–15 minutes, removing from the oven as soon as the edges start to brown. Cool for 2–3 minutes before carefully lifting from the tins onto cooling racks.

**6** Serve warm, dusted with icing sugar. (See photo on p 18).

# Filo Mincemeat Triangles

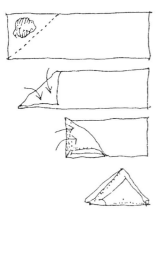

**1** Each Christmas we make some of these quickly-made triangles. Because the mincemeat has not been thickened, the mincemeat triangles shout to be eaten less than an hour after they are baked.

**2** Lightly brush with melted butter then stack three sheets of fresh filo pastry. Cut these crosswise into 3–5 strips. At one end of each strip put a spoonful of mincemeat.

**3** Fold the filo over the filling forming a triangle. Keep folding to form triangle pastries, enclosing filling completely.

**4** Brush with more melted butter.

**5** Bake at 180°C for about 10 minutes or until golden brown. Serve warm rather than hot, dusted with icing sugar.

# Christmas Mincemeat Muffins

Although mince pies are nice, making their crust can be time consuming, especially when there are other Christmas chores waiting. Why not put spoonfuls of mixture in muffins instead. Serve these warm, and wait for the compliments!

**For 12 medium muffins:**

1¾ cups self-raising flour

¾ cup caster sugar

½ tsp salt

2 eggs

½ cup sour cream

½ cup milk

½ tsp rum, whisky or brandy essence

½ cup Christmas Mincemeat (page 19)

**1** Measure the first three ingredients into a large bowl, and stir with a fork.

**2** In another bowl, mix together with a whisk, until smooth, the eggs, sour cream, milk and essence of your choice.

**3** Without overmixing, add the liquids to the dry ingredients. Coat 12 medium sized muffin pans with non-stick spray and half fill the 12 pans with the mixture. Using a dampened teaspoon, make a small indentation on the top of each, and into it put 1–2 teaspoons of the mincemeat. Cover each with a spoonful of the remaining mixture trying to cover the "enclosed" mincemeat.

**4** Bake at 200°C for about 12–15 minutes or until golden brown. The centres should spring back when pressed.

**5** Serve warm, for Christmas Day breakfast or brunch, or with coffee at any time of the day over the holiday period. Serve hot for dessert between Christmas and New Year with fresh berries and icecream or whipped cream or with Rum and Brandy Butters (see page 27).

# Traditional Christmas Pudding

This recipe is similar to one made by Alison's mother and aunts. Make it well in advance (freezing if you like) and have it ready to boil up again on Christmas Day

## For 8–12 servings:

2 cups flour

75g butter

½ cup brown sugar

1 cup raisins

1 cup currants

1 cup sultanas

¼ cup minced peel

¼ cup cherries

1 tsp cinnamon

1 tsp mixed spice

½ cup golden syrup

½ cup milk

1 tsp baking soda

2 eggs

grated rind of 1 orange

grated rind of 1 lemon

**1** Mix together in a large basin the flour, butter and brown sugar, rubbing the butter into the flour. Add this to the fruit which has been washed, then dried in the oven or another warm place. Stir in the spices.

**2** Warm the golden syrup and add it to the milk with the baking soda dissolved in it, the eggs and the finely grated citrus rind. Beat with a fork until well mixed. Pour the egg mixture into the dry ingredients and fruit. Mix well.

**3** Butter or spray a large basin and pour the mixture into it, leaving enough space for the pudding to rise as it cooks. Cover the basin with its lid or several layers of greaseproof paper tied firmly in place with string, or with foil. Place on a rack or a saucer in a large saucepan, half-filled with boiling water. Put a lid on the saucepan and boil gently for 3–4 hours.

**4** Check frequently to see that the pudding has not boiled dry. When necessary, add more boiling water.

**5** After the pudding has boiled, remove it from its basin and leave to cool on a wire rack. When cold, wrap in aluminium foil or a plastic bag and keep it in a cool dry place until it is needed. (Alison stores her pudding in the bottom of the refrigerator.)

**6** When the pudding is to be used, unwrap it, sprinkle it with sherry, whisky or brandy, replace it in the basin with a light covering and steam it again for 1–3 hours (the longer the better).

**7** Serve hot with the sauce of your choice (see page 27).

# Individual Christmas Puddings

**Use small bowls or teacups which hold ½ cup of water. (This is a good way to use cups with broken handles).**

**1** Make the Christmas Pudding mixture, and spray the insides of the half-cup containers (about six of them) with non-stick spray.

**2** Spoon the uncooked mixture into the small bowls or cups, making sure you don't have any big air spaces. Level the tops so each cup is about ¾ full.

**3** Put a 10cm square of cling-wrap loosely over each cup, and arrange the bowls in a circle quite close to the edge of the microwave oven.

**4** Cook for 12–14 minutes on Medium High (70% power), or until the puddings spring back when pressed.

**5** Leave for 5 minutes before turning out the mini puddings.

**6** Serve with any of the sauces on page 27.

# To serve with your Christmas Pudding

To "flame" a Christmas pudding, heat 1–2 tablespoons of brandy, whisky or rum to bath temperature. Pour it over the hot pudding and set alight. The brandy will not burn unless it is heated first. (The flame may not be visible unless the room is in darkness).

## Mary Alice's Rum Butter

This delicious "sauce" makes any steamed pudding very special! Try it as a topping for mincemeat pies or muffins too. Make extra, for gifts for good friends!

100g softened butter

1 cup brown sugar

1 tsp freshly grated nutmeg

2 Tbsp rum

Beat or process all the ingredients until light and creamy. Cover and refrigerate to store for up to a month. Serve at room temperature.

## Brandy Butter

This very rich sauce should be eaten in small amounts!

125g softened butter

2 cups icing sugar

1 Tbsp brandy

Beat or process all ingredients until light and creamy. Refrigerate until the butter hardens. Pile into a serving dish and serve at room temperature. For individual servings, chill the mixture until easy to handle, roll into walnut-sized balls, then refrigerate until required.

**Variation:** For hard sauce with a slightly grainy texture, replace the icing sugar with 1 cup of caster sugar.

## Creamy Custard Sauce

A less rich alternative!

¼ cup custard powder

¼ cup brown sugar

1 egg

3 cups milk

1 tsp vanilla

2 Tbsp butter

1 Tbsp brandy or 2 Tbsp rum, optional

Stir custard powder and sugar together in a pot. Add the egg and mix again.

Stir in the milk and vanilla, cook over a medium heat, stirring constantly. When the milk is hot, add the butter. As soon as the custard thickens and bubbles, remove from the heat and add the brandy. Serve warm.

# Christmas Pudding Truffles

We like these truffles dressed up so that they look like mini-Christmas puddings. If you feel that this is too time-consuming, serve them as plain truffles rolled in coconut. They taste very good both ways.

1 cup currants

2 tsp very finely grated orange or tangelo rind

¼ cup rum, whisky, brandy or citrus juice

250g (2½ cups) crumbs from a chocolate or plain cake

125g (⅝ cup) chocolate chips

**For decoration:**

75g white chocolate

1 tsp oil

about 6 red cherries

about 6 green cherries

**1** Put the currants in a sieve and pour boiling water through them, then put them in a bowl with the very finely grated rind from a tangelo or orange, and the spirit of your choice or the same amount of juice from the orange or tangelo.

**2** Leave the currants to stand while you crumb the cake, and then melt the chocolate chips, heating until liquid. This will take about 4–5 minutes on Medium in a microwave oven, and a little longer in a large metal bowl standing over a pot of hot but not boiling water. When the chocolate has melted, stir into it the crumbs, then the currant mixture.

**3** Mix well together, then roll into small, walnut-sized balls, or balls which will fit nicely in small foil or fluted paper confectionery cups. (Roll in coconut if not decorating further.) Refrigerate until cold.

**4** Warm pieces of white chocolate with the oil in a clean bowl, in a microwave oven for about 3 minutes on Medium or over hot water, as before. Stir until smooth.

**5** Chop the cherries. Have red cherry pieces chunky, and the green pieces pointed like leaves.

**6** Spoon a little of the warm white mixture on top of a little pudding, helping it to look as if it is flowing, if necessary.

**7** This takes a little experience, but is mainly a matter of having the truffle cold and the melted mixture semi-liquid. Before the white chocolate sets, put about three little red berries in the middle of the icing, and a couple of green leaves around them.

# Christmas Tree Biscuits

**Try making these rock-hard Christmas Tree biscuits with your children. The uncooked dough tastes wonderful, so do not expect the impossible!**

50g butter

1 cup honey

¾ cup brown sugar

1 Tbsp lemon juice

1 Tbsp finely grated lemon rind

2 tsp cinnamon

1 tsp ground cloves

1 tsp nutmeg

1 tsp allspice

½ tsp baking soda

3–4 cups flour

**1** Measure all the ingredients except the baking soda and flour into a medium-sized saucepan. Stir over a low heat until all the ingredients are blended and the sugar is no longer grainy. Do not boil. Remove from the heat and cool to room temperature.

**2** Stir in the baking soda sifted with 1 cup of the flour. Stir well then add more flour, about half a cup at a time, until the dough is firm enough to roll out on a floured board. The more flour you add the harder and longer lasting the biscuits will be.

**3** Roll out dough to about 5mm thick and cut into interesting shapes, using biscuit cutters etc. Before cooking, pierce a hole to thread red ribbon or wool through later. (A gently twisted straw makes good holes).

**4** Bake at 170°C for about 10-20 minutes, or longer, until the edges brown lightly. (Longer baked biscuits are harder.)

**5** Cool on a rack. Leave plain or decorate as desired with water icing, or make an icing of piping consistency, adding water and a little butter to icing sugar, and pipe designs on to the cooked biscuits. If you don't have an icing nozzle, you can put your icing mixture into a strong plastic bag then snip a very small hole in one corner.

# Shortbread Shapes

Shortbread, with its distinctive texture and buttery flavour, is a traditional Christmas treat. When you use decorative cutters instead of making squares or rectangles, your shortbread will be extra special!

220g butter

½ cup caster sugar

2 cups sifted flour

1 cup cornflour, stirred

**1** Cream the butter, then add the caster sugar and beat until light and fluffy. Sift the flour before measuring it, then spoon it lightly into the cup measure without packing it down. Add with the cornflour to the creamed mixture, mix thoroughly then chill the dough if it is too soft to roll.

**2** Roll out on a floured board, 7.5mm–1cm thick.

**3** Cut into shapes with cutters, or into rectangles, rounds (with the top of a glass) and squares, and bake on baking paper or a Teflon liner, at 150°C for 15–20 minutes. Watch carefully towards the end of the cooking time and take shortbread from the oven as soon as the edges change colour slightly.

**4** Cool on a rack. Store in airtight containers when cold. Freeze if keeping for more than two weeks, before giving away as a gift.

**5** For a relatively inexpensive and attractive presentation, arrange shortbread on a Christmassy paper plate (with or without a doily) then slip the plate into a cellophane "envelope" which you can seal completely with transparent tape.

# Almond Rosettes

For a present for someone special, fill a decorative glass jar, with a tight fitting lid, with these pretty biscuits. If you don't have a forcing bag, shape them by pushing through a heavy weight plastic bag with the corner cut out.

## For 24–36 biscuits:

2 egg whites

¼ cup plus 1 Tbsp caster sugar

125g ground almonds

¼–½ tsp almond essence

¼ tsp salt

8–16 glacé cherries

**1** Put the first five ingredients into a food processor. Mix until well blended and fairly smooth. If the mixture looks too soft to keep its shape at the end of this time, add more ground almonds.

**2** Vary the amount of almond essence, depending on its strength. The biscuits should taste definitely, but not strongly, of almonds.

**3** Spray an oven slide thickly with non-stick spray, or use a Teflon liner, since these biscuits stick easily. Pipe or otherwise shape them into rosettes, making 24–36 biscuits. As the biscuits do not rise during cooking, you can put them quite close together.

**4** Cut the cherries into halves or quarters, and press them into the uncooked biscuit dough.

**5** Bake at 180°C for about 20 minutes, until the biscuits are golden brown all over. If they appear to be turning brown too soon, turn the oven down to 170°C.

**6** Cool on a rack, then store in airtight jars. These biscuits will stay nice and crisp for about a month if stored in an airtight container.

**7** To make these without a food processor, beat the egg whites until bubbly but not stiff, add the remaining ingredients, and beat well with a wooden spoon until the mixture becomes quite stiff.

# Custard Kisses

We can think of nothing nicer than being given a batch of small custard kisses as a gift – in a pretty box or jar, or packed as a Christmas Cracker in a tube. Lovely!

## For 25 kisses:

175g butter

¾ cup icing sugar

1 tsp vanilla essence

1½ cups flour

½ cup custard powder

1 tsp baking powder

## Icing:

2 Tbsp butter

½ cup icing sugar

1 Tbsp custard powder

few drops of vanilla essence

**1** Soften but do not melt the butter. Cream with the icing sugar and vanilla, then stir in the sifted flour, custard powder and baking powder. Mix well, then form the mixture into about 50 small balls. Flatten these in your hand before you put them on a lightly sprayed oven tray, then make a pattern with a dampened fork, the dimpled surface of a meat hammer, or the bottom of a patterned glass.

**2** OR form the mixture into a cylinder and refrigerate until it will cut without flattening. Cut slices from the cylinder, put on a tray and decorate as above.

**3** Bake at 170°C–180°C for 12–15 minutes, depending on the thickness of the biscuits. When done, they should feel firm but not have browned. Cool on a rack.

**4** Stick cold biscuits together with icing made by mixing together softened (but not melted) butter and the other icing ingredients.

**5** Store biscuits in airtight tins once the icing has set. Freeze if desired.

# Chocolate Truffles

100g wine biscuit crumbs

100g butter

¼ cup cocoa

1 cup icing sugar

½ cup coconut

2 Tbsp sherry

**1** Put the biscuits in a plastic bag and bang with a rolling pin until completely crushed.

**2** Soften, but do not melt the butter. Add cocoa, icing sugar, coconut, sherry and crushed biscuits. Stir well, and cool the mixture for 10 minutes in the refrigerator before rolling it into small balls.

**3** Roll the balls in extra coconut.

**4** Store in refrigerator or freezer.

# Fabulous Fudge

100g butter

1 cup sugar

¼ cup golden syrup

400g can condensed milk

1 tsp vanilla

**1** Mix all ingredients except vanilla in a microwave bowl resistant to high heat.

**2** Microwave on High for 10–12 minutes, stirring every 2 minutes until all sugar has dissolved, mixture has bubbled vigorously all over surface, and a little dropped in cold water forms a soft ball.

**3** Add vanilla. Beat for about 5 minutes, until mixture loses its gloss. Before it sets firm, spoon into a lightly buttered or sprayed 20cm square pan. When firm, cut into squares.

# Uncooked Coconut Ice

**Let your children make this Coconut Ice for someone special, then reward yourself with our Fabulous Fudge!**

½ of a (400g) can condensed milk

2 cups desiccated coconut

2 cups icing sugar

1 tsp vanilla essence

¼ tsp raspberry essence

4–6 drops red food colouring

**1** Warm can of condensed milk if cold. Measure into fairly large bowl (or food processor bowl). Add coconut, icing sugar and vanilla. Mix until combined.

**2** Remove half mixture and press out 1cm thick on extra coconut on board. To remaining mixture, add raspberry essence and enough food colouring to make a medium pink. Press this over the white layer. Chill until firm for 15–20 minutes, then cut into squares.

**3** Refrigerate or freeze.

# Easy Chocolate Fudge

500g dark chocolate

400g can condensed milk

½ tsp vanilla

walnut halves to decorate, optional

**1** Break up the chocolate if necessary. Heat the condensed milk with the broken chocolate in a heavy saucepan, over a low heat, or in a microwave oven on Medium, stirring frequently until the chocolate is melted and the two are well blended.

**2** Add the vanilla, stir well and pour into 20cm square cake tin lined with baking paper or a Teflon liner.

**3** Leave until firm, then cut into 8 strips crosswise and lengthways. Top pieces with a walnut half if desired.

**4** Cover and refrigerate or freeze.

# Spiced Almonds

A nicely decorated jar of carefully seasoned, roasted nuts is always a welcome gift. Choose your decorations and seasonings to suit the recipient!

1 cup (150g) almonds

2 tsp egg white

¼ cup caster sugar

1 tsp cinnamon

1 tsp mixed spice

¼ tsp ground cloves

pinch salt

**1** Put the (dry) nuts into a large bowl. Add the measured egg white which has been beaten very lightly with a fork.

**2** Using your fingers, coat the nuts with the egg. Leave to stand for 4–5 minutes, until the nuts soak up some of the egg and have only a 'tacky' surface.

**3** Meanwhile, mix the caster sugar with the remaining ingredients. Put half of this mixture in with the nuts, shake to coat lightly, then arrange nuts in one layer on a Teflon liner or baking paper on an oven slide.

**4** Shake or finely sieve more coating mixture over nuts (do not turn nuts over).

**5** Bake at 125°C (without a fan if possible) for 15 minutes. When cool, transfer to airtight jars, plastic or cellophane bags.

# Christmas Pickle

Alison named this pickle for its festive colours. She often gives it to friends at Christmas as it tastes so good with cold meats. It turns cheese and crackers into something special, and is useful when unexpected guests call.

8 cups diced telegraph cucumber

¼ cup plain salt

4 onions, diced

2–3 red peppers, diced

3 cups sugar

1 tsp celery seed

1 tsp mustard seed

2 cups wine vinegar

2–3 Tbsp cornflour

**1** Halve cucumbers lengthwise then scoop out and discard the central seedy part, using a teaspoon. Without removing the peel, cut cucumber flesh into small, evenly shaped cubes.

**2** Measure cucumber into a glass, plastic, china or stainless steel container. Sprinkle with salt and leave to stand for 30 minutes, stirring several times. Drain and rinse, discarding the liquid.

**3** Cut the onions and peppers into cubes the same size as the cucumber. Put prepared cucumber, onion, peppers, sugar, celery and mustard seeds into a large saucepan. Bring to the boil stirring constantly. Mix cornflour with a little extra vinegar and stir into the cucumber mixture.

**4** Pour into hot jars that have been cleaned and heated in the oven. If jars have plastic screw lids or lacquered metal lids, pour boiling water over them and leave to stand for a few minutes, then screw them on to the hot jars of pickle.

**5** For jars without lids, cover cool pickle with melted paraffin (or candle) wax, then with cellophane tops.

**Note:** A 2 litre icecream container holds exactly 8 cups of cubed cucumber.

Pickles which are stored in the refrigerator do not need to be sealed.

Merry Christmas

# Sweetcorn Pickle

1 cup chopped celery

1 cup chopped onion

1 red pepper, chopped

1 green pepper, chopped

1 tsp celery seed

1 tsp turmeric

1½ cups wine vinegar

4 cups canned corn

¾ cup sugar

1 Tbsp cornflour

2 tsp dry mustard

2 tsp salt

**1** Measure the first seven ingredients into a large saucepan. Boil for 5 minutes then add the corn. Bring back to the boil.

**2** Mix the sugar, cornflour, mustard and salt to a thin cream with a little more vinegar, stir in and bring back to the boil again. Simmer for 2 minutes, stirring constantly, then bottle. Top with metal lids or preserving seals.

## Sealing Pickles and Chutney

**Pickles and chutney which will be eaten in a few weeks may be refrigerated in jars with screw lids. For longer storage, see below.**

**1** Boil the jars and lids for about 5 minutes. Pour the very hot pickles into the hot, empty jars to within 1 cm of the tops of the jars.

**2** Wipe the rim of the jar clean with a sterilised cloth.

**3** Without touching the underside of the lid, put it on the hot jar of pickle, and screw on tightly.

**4** Leave to stand on a wooden board or chopping board until cool.

**5** If the jar lids "pop" down as the pickles or chutney cools, you know they have sealed and may be kept at room temperature for 1–2 years. Jars without "popped" lids should be refrigerated, and the contents eaten within a month or so.

# Index

Published by
Hyndman Publishing
PO Box 19, Amberley,
North Canterbury

**ISBN:**
1-877382-75-2

**TEXT:**
©Simon & Alison Holst

**DESIGN:**
Rob Di Leva

**SANTA ILLUSTRATIONS:**
Alison Holst

**FOOD STYLING:**
Simon Holst

**PHOTOGRAPHY:**
Lindsay Keats

**HOME ECONOMISTS:**
Simon & Alison Holst,
Michelle Gill

The recipes in this book have been carefully tested by the authors. The publisher and the authors have made every effort to ensure that the instructions are accurate and safe, but they cannot accept liability for any resulting injury or loss or damage to property, whether direct or consequential.

Because ovens and microwave ovens vary so much, you should take the cooking times suggested in recipes as guides only. The first time you make a recipe, check it at intervals to make sure it is not cooking faster, or more slowly than expected.

Always follow the detailed instructions given by manufacturers of your appliances and equipment, rather than the more general instructions given in these recipes.

# Cooking for
## Christmas

Christmas is a time for happy gatherings of family and friends, the exchange of gifts and the enjoyment of good food. Most of us remember fondly the traditional foods which our mothers and grandmothers produced each year.

Simon and Alison are confident the recipes in this book will inspire you to cook your own Christmas meals and treats and that you will enjoy making them. Many of the foods can be made some time before Christmas and there are great recipes for attractive food gifts to put under your Christmas tree.

Treat your family and friends to:

- Delicious, moist Christmas cakes
- Festive roast chicken and fabulous glazed ham
- Beautiful biscotti and biscuits
- Panforte
- Colourful Christmas pickles
- Fabulous fudges and other sweet treats
- Traditional Christmas puddings
- Spicy fruit mincemeat and Christmas mince pies
  and much more!

Simon and Dame Alison Holst's combined talents make them a formidable team. They have written over 30 cookbooks together which have quickly become best sellers. These books have sold over 1.9 million copies to date.

ISBN 1-877382-75-2

9 781877 382758 >

HYNDMAN PUBLISHING